SIMPLE TECHNOLOGY

WHEELS

Liz Lennon and Ellie O'Shea

WINDMILL BOOKS

Published in 2026 by Windmill Books,
an Imprint of Rosen Publishing
2544 Clinton St.
Buffalo, NY 14224

First published in Great Britain in 2023 by Wayland

Editor: Sarah Peutrill
Designer: Lisa Peacock
Science consultant: Peter Riley

Cataloging-in-Publication Data
Names: Lennon, Liz, author. | O'Shea, Ellie, illustrator.
Title: Wheels / by Liz Lennon, illustrated by Ellie O'Shea.
Description: Buffalo, NY : Windmill Books, 2026. | Series: Simple technology | Includes glossary and index.
Identifiers: ISBN 9781725397132 (pbk.) | ISBN 9781725397149 (library bound) | ISBN 9781725397156 (ebook)
Subjects: LCSH: Wheels--Juvenile literature. | Axles--Juvenile literature.
Classification: LCC TJ181.5 L46 2026 | DDC 621.8--dc23

Printed in China

CPSIA Compliance Information: Batch #QW26WM
For Further Information contact Rosen Publishing at 1-800-237-9932

CONTENTS

WHAT ARE WHEELS?

Wheels are simple machines. A machine is something we use to make work easier to do. Wheels are shaped like a circle. Here are some things that have wheels.

Roller skates

Toy train

Tricycle

Wheels are good for rolling along and moving things. Which of these has another job to do? Find out on page 21.

Pizza cutter

Wheelchair

Wheelbarrow

WHEELS AND AXLES

Wheels are a disc that can be made from metal, plastic, or other materials. Some are covered in a tire. Some wheels have spokes. This makes them less heavy than a solid disc.

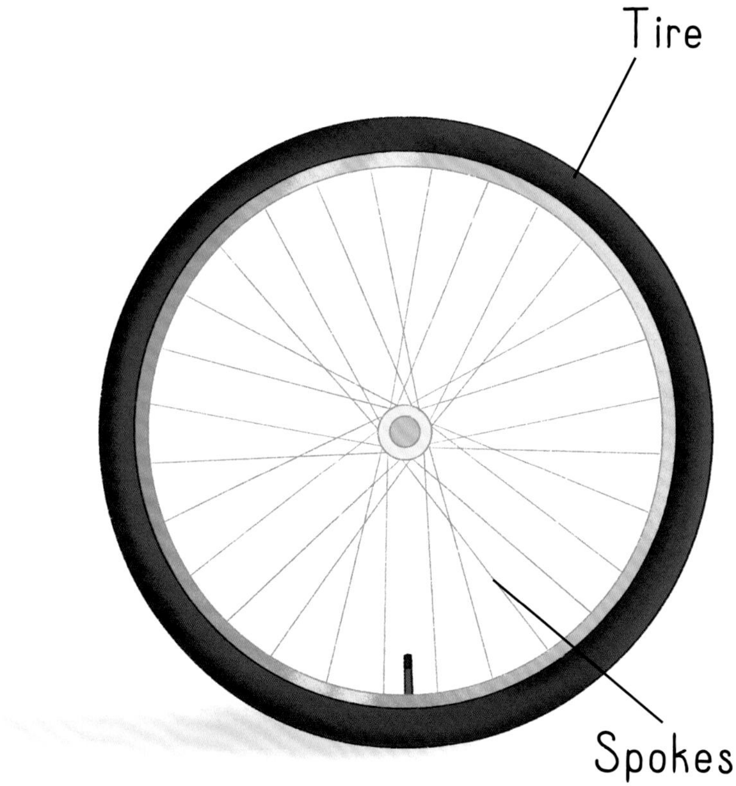

Wheels have to turn around on a rod. The rod is called an axle.

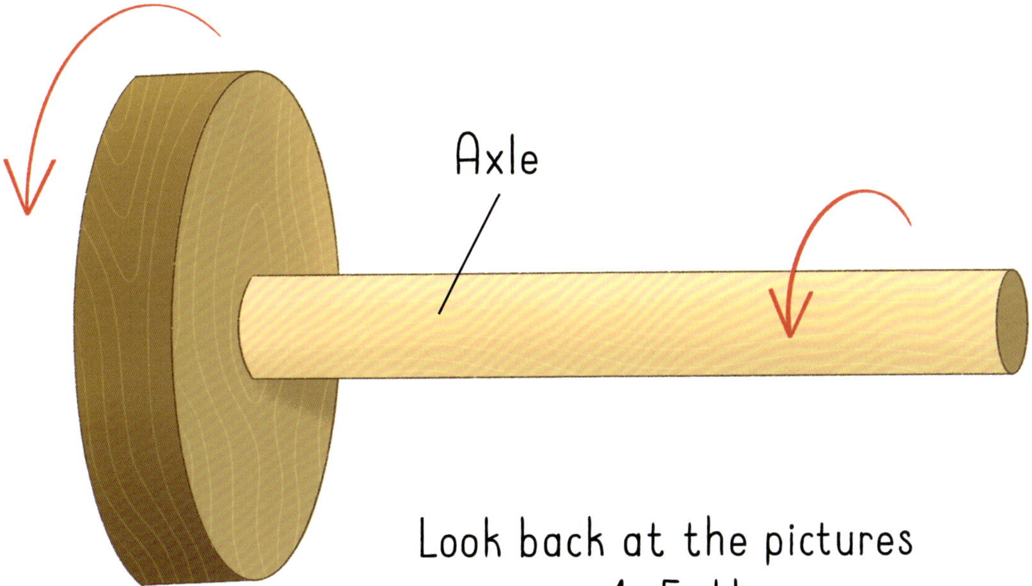

Look back at the pictures on pages 4–5. How many axles do you think each machine has? The answer is on page 32.

MOVING THINGS

Wheels are helpful for moving things around.

Josh has a heavy box to move. It's hard work to pull it. It drags on the ground, which makes a pull called friction.

Now Josh is using a cart with wheels to help. The wheels help to reduce the friction. They roll along the ground. That's easier!

DIFFERENT TYPES OF WHEEL

Look around when you go outside. There are wheels everywhere. They are all different shapes and sizes. Some are thick and some are thin.

Why do you think the wheels on the truck are so big?

TURNING AND STEERING

As well as moving things along, wheels can help with turning and steering.

A door knob is a wheel too. The axle is inside the door.

MAKING A TOY CAR

Luna has made a toy car. The body is made from a clothes pin. What are the wheels made from?

How many axles are there on Luna's toy car?

What could you use to make a toy car?

TIRES

Vehicle wheels are covered with tires that are made of rubber and pumped full of air.

The tires make traveling more comfortable. It cushions you from hard and bumpy surfaces.

Tires have a pattern on them called tread. This works like the tread on the bottom of your sneakers. This helps the vehicle to grip the road surface.

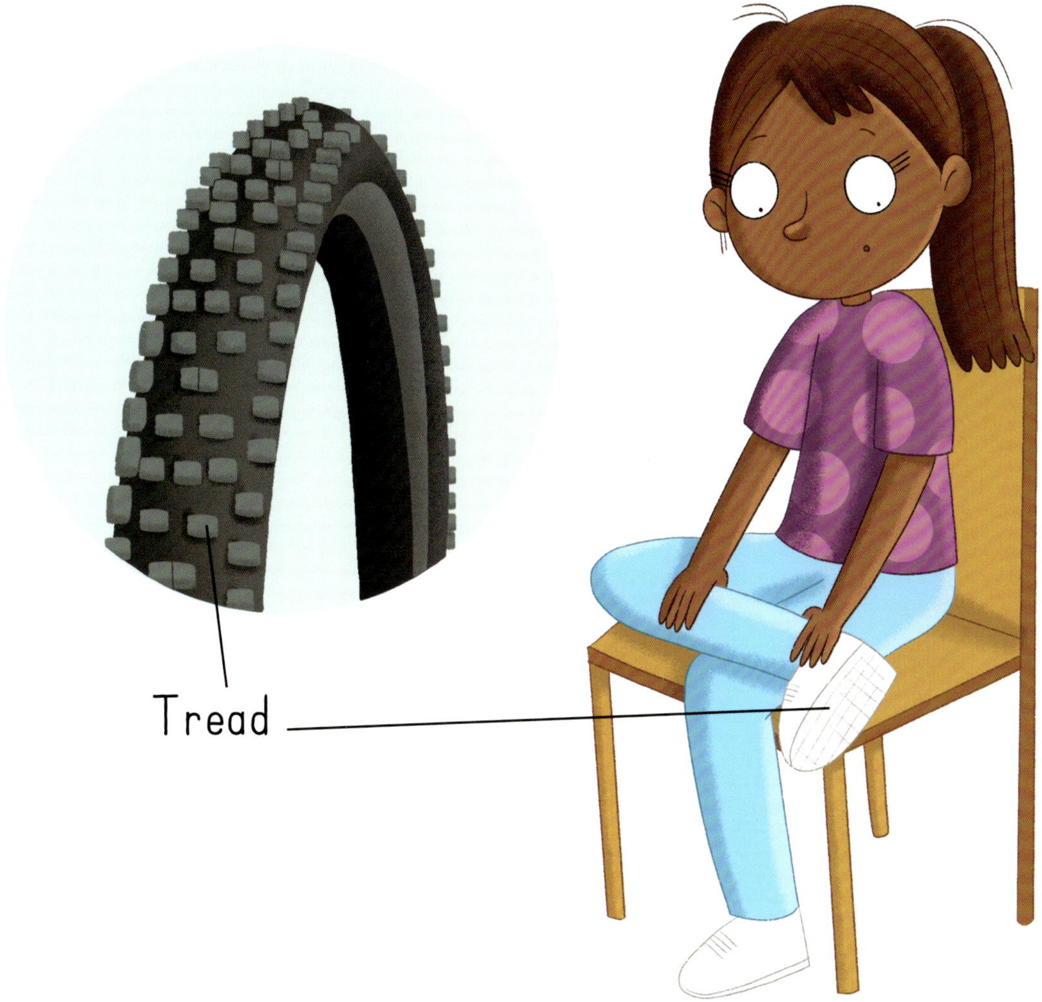

TRACTOR

This tractor has huge wheels and there is a big tread on its tires. The huge wheels hold the heavy tractor steady. The big tread helps the tractor drive through thick, sticky mud.

WORKING WHEELS

We use wheels in other ways. This water wheel moves water to generate power.

This wheel helps
the potter to work
with clay.

This wheel is used
to cut up pizza.

SPINNING WHEELS

These wheels are for fun! A carousel is a spinning wheel you have probably been on. Can you find the axle?

This Ferris wheel is at a fairground.

GEARS

A gear is a wheel with teeth around its edge called cogs. A gear can be used to turn another gear. Look at the gears below. Which way do you think the red gear will turn? The answer is on page 32.

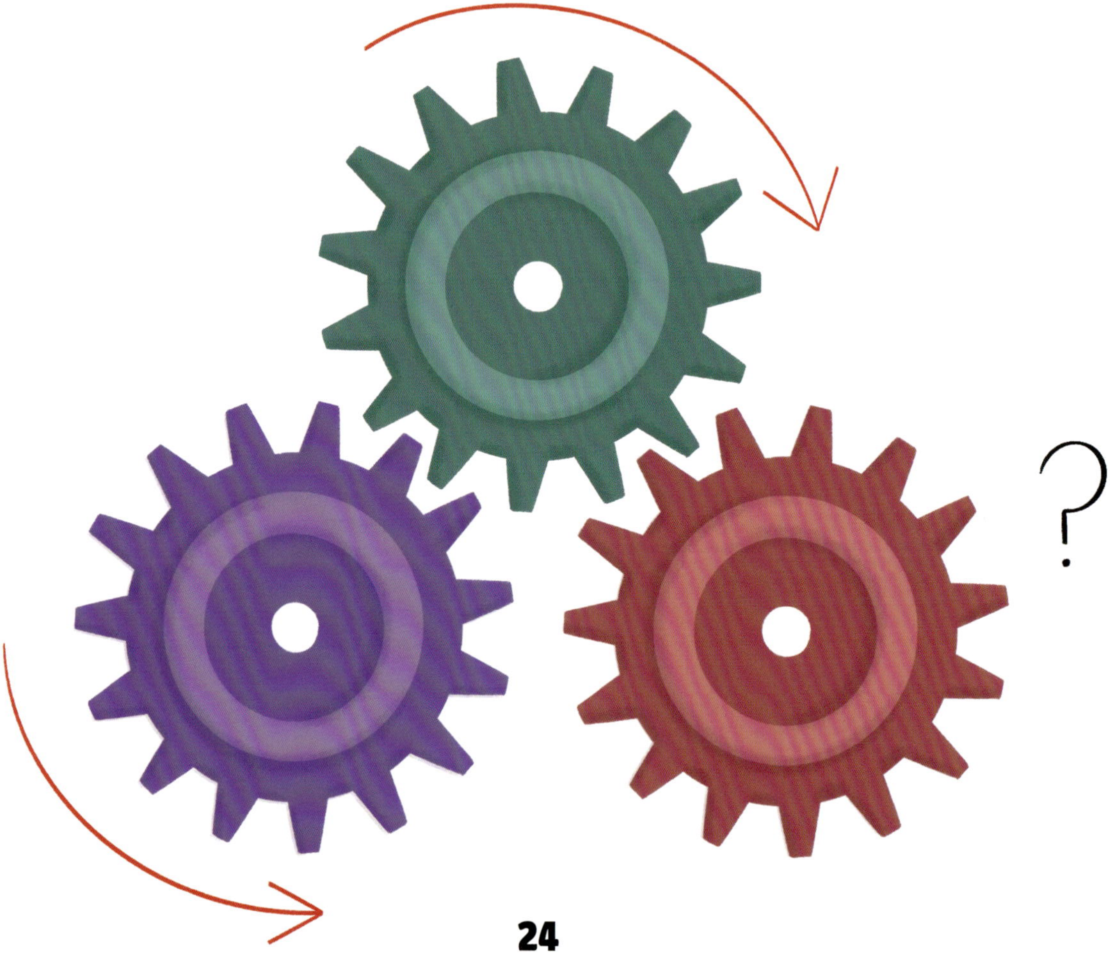

When a small gear turns a large gear, the large gear gets a bigger push.

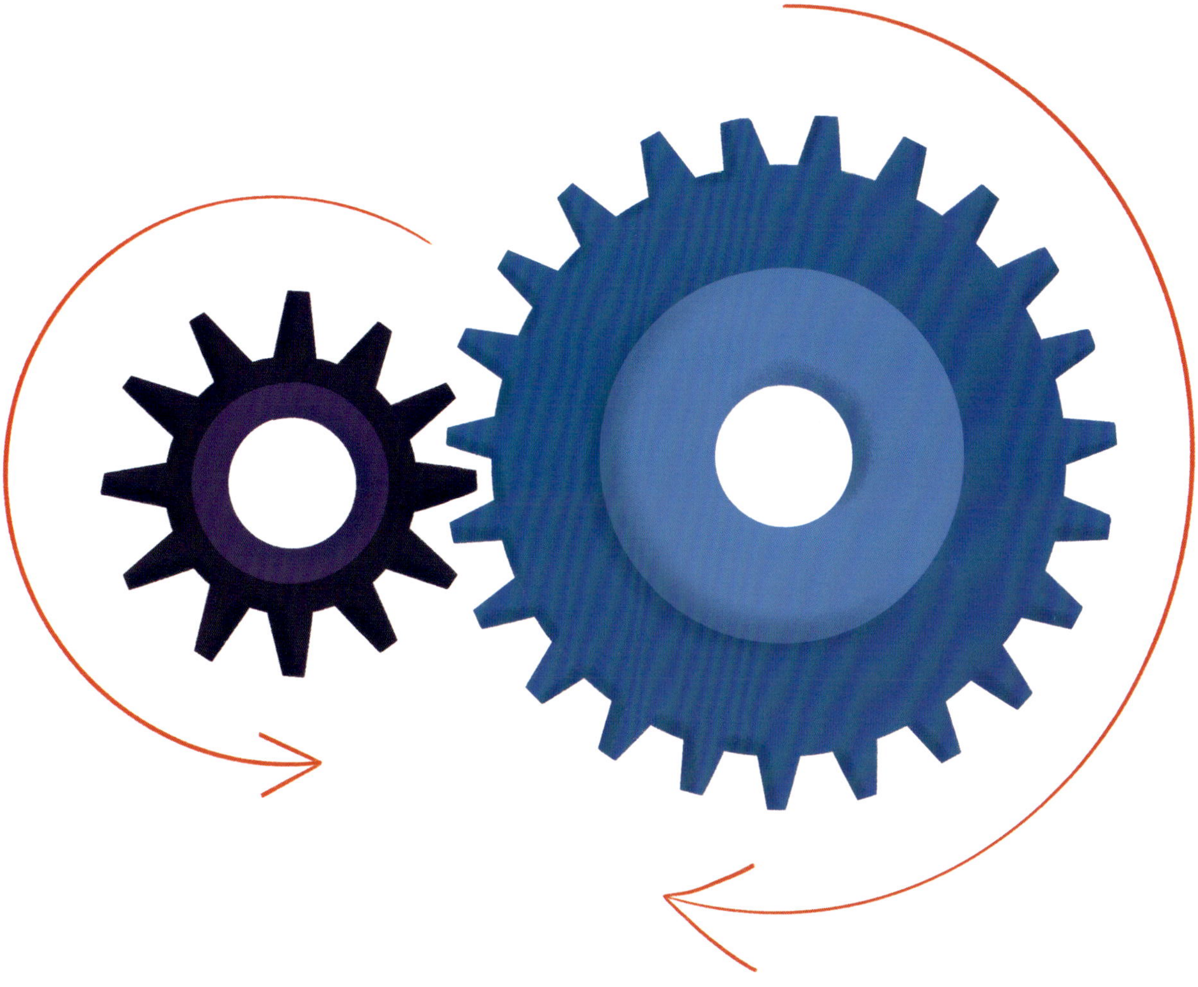

MACHINES WITH GEARS

These machines have wheels with gears. Can you find them in the pictures?

Watch

Bicycle

WHEELS AND PEOPLE

People have been using wheels
for over 5,000 years.

Today, wheels have changed quite a bit. We make them from new materials. They have tires and spokes.

But, they are still the same simple machines that people invented to help them move things along.

GLOSSARY

Here are the key words we explored in this book. Try covering the meanings to see if you can remember them yourself. Were you right?

Axle a rod that two wheels turn on.

Force a push or a pull.

Gear a wheel with teeth around it called cogs.

Friction a force that occurs when an object rubs against a surface.

Machine anything that helps us by taking a force and transferring it to where it is needed.

Material the thing that something is made from, such as tires are made from rubber.

Rubber a material that comes from trees and can also be manufactured.

Spoke each of the rods that attach the center of a wheel to its outer edge.

Tread the thick, raised part of a tire that helps a bike, car, or other vehicle grip the road.

Vehicle a type of transportation such as a bike, car, or truck.

Wheel a circular frame that turns on an axle.

INDEX

ANSWERS

Page 7: Roller skates have two axles each; the toy train and tricycle have two axles each; the pizza cutter, wheelchair, and wheelbarrow have one axle each.

Page 24:

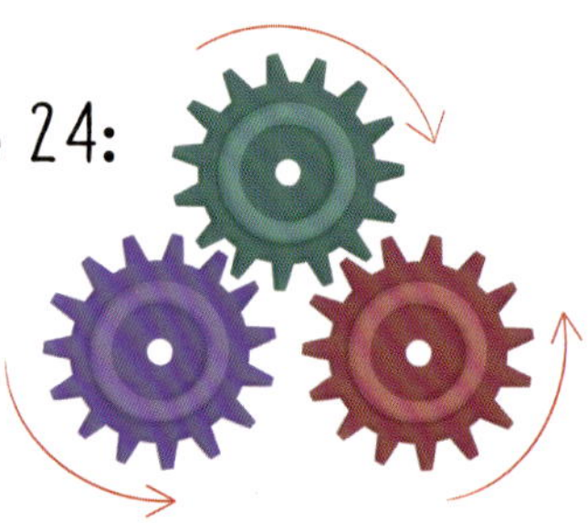